The POWER OF KINDNESS

MAC ANDERSON

simple truths®

Design and production: Koechel Peterson & Associate, Inc., Minneapolis, MN
Edited by: Alice Patenaude
All images provide by Thinkstock and Shutterstock.

Published by Simple Truths, an imprint of Sourcebooks, Inc.
P.O. Box 4410, Naperville, Illinois 60567-4410
(630) 961-3900
Fax: (630) 961-2168
www.sourcebooks.com

Printed and bound in China.
OGP 10 9 8 7 6 5 4 3 2

✳ TABLE OF CONTENTS ✳

"WE MAKE A LIVING BY WHAT WE GET.
WE MAKE A LIFE BY WHAT WE GIVE."

~WINSTON CHURCHILL

INTRODUCTION

I RECENTLY WROTE a book titled, **Customer Love**, where I shared this story about Captain Denny Flanagan:

As flight cancellations and delays wreak havoc on weary travelers, and planes are fuller than ever, the Wall Street Journal has managed to find a bright spot—United Airlines Captain Denny Flanagan.

On a flight headed your way, there is a pilot who is literally a gift from the heavens. For 21 years now, Flanagan, a former Navy pilot, has put the friendly in friendly skies.

With his sense of humor and personal touch, he individually welcomes aboard every passenger on his United Airlines' plane.

"*You have not lived a perfect day, even though you have earned your money, unless you have done something for someone who will never be able to repay you.*"

RUTH SMELTZER

The POWER OF
KINDNESS

A father of five, Flanagan has also been known to buy food for planeloads of passengers on delayed flights. He snaps photos of dogs in the cargo hold to show owners their pets are safe and calls the parents of children traveling alone.

"I want to treat them like I treat my family and it works. It's like hospitality. You stand at the door and you greet people when they come in and you say goodbye on the porch and wave to them," said Flanagan, who is 56 and lives in Ohio.

His unique brand of hospitality includes sending handwritten notes to frequent flyers and raffling off bottles of wine.

"How 'bout that? A bottle of chilled chardonnay from a pilot," said a delighted Paul Schroeder, a lucky United passenger.

He has developed quite a following in the air and online. One of the many posts on FlyerTalk.com about Flanagan read, "His effort rubbed off on the crew too, they were great."

Attitudes are truly contagious, and Captain Flanagan's is certainly worth catching!

But here, as the late Paul Harvey always said, is ..."the rest of the story."

Not long after the book's release, I received a call from Captain Flanagan, who said, "Mac, I loved your book about customer service and I just wanted to thank you for including my story." We talked for about 15 minutes and when I hung up, I knew that Denny Flanagan was "real," and very passionate about not only being a good Captain for United Airlines, but making a positive difference in the world.

The next day, I sent Denny a signed copy of the book, thanking him for making a difference and here is the letter I got back:

Dear Mac:

Thank you for my personal signed copy of **Customer Love**. I am honored to be included with the 24 other great stories of customer service. People try to make service complicated, but it's really not rocket science. The recipe has two ingredients: choose your attitude each morning and anticipate your customer's needs.

In fact, one of the things that I've enjoyed doing over the years is having dinner with my customers during my long layovers. It just gives me the opportunity to know their needs and determine ways we can serve them better. It also allows me to introduce my first officers to our customers, to show them how they can make a difference when they become captains.

From a dinner with one customer I have now expanded it to having dinner with 20 customers. I frequently get asked by customers how they can book one of my flights. At first, I just let it roll off my shoulders as a silly comment, but when they kept asking, I posted one of my upcoming flights on FlyerTalk. com and 26 people booked it as a result of that post. I guess I'll need a bigger table for this one!

After I received Denny's letter, I called to thank him again for being a great example for all of us to follow and during our conversation he said this:

"After the *Wall Street Journal* article came out, I was called by Ellen DeGeneres about coming on her show. During the call, she said, 'Captain, what do you want out of this?' Without hesitation, I said, 'I want a national holiday.' She laughed. And then I said, 'I want a national holiday called NICE. Why? Because at least once a year, everyone would be reminded how good it feels to be NICE to one another!'"

I then said, "Denny, I'm on board!"

Now here's the deal. I'm an optimist, but even an optimist knows that national holidays are tough to come by. But I've always lived by the, "nothing ventured, nothing gained" philosophy. Gandhi's simple, but profound words put everything into perspective,

"Be the change you wish to see in the world."

You see, in my mind and in Denny's mind, the word NICE is joined at the hip with the word kindness. Almost every religion in the world has kindness, front and center. In fact, Mark Twain said, "It's the one language we can all understand…even the blind can see it and the deaf can hear it."

So here's the question to ponder…why aren't more people kind?

I'm not sure I know the answer, but I think I do. My guess is that almost everyone understands the power of kindness…because we've all been on the receiving end and we know how it can make us feel. But for whatever reason, many people haven't been inspired enough to make it part of their everyday life. It hasn't reached the top of an already crowded priority list.

That's what this little book is all about; to move "random acts of kindness" up a few notches on your priority list, by sharing inspirational stories like Denny Flanagan's and many others. Because once you have the desire to make kindness a bigger part of your life, my hope is that you'll truly realize that what

Emerson said is the key to real happiness. . ."One of the most beautiful compensations in life is that no man can help another without helping himself." In fact, how do you feel when you open the door for someone, and they smile and say "thank you?" You feel good about yourself because you're being kind.

Of course, I'm living in the real world and I don't expect everyone to be a "Denny Flanagan." Denny's way is "his way," but we're all unique beings, with our "own way" to leave our mark of kindness on the world…be it large or small. All I know for sure is that if this little book inspires every person who reads it to perform one random act of kindness that you wouldn't have otherwise, the world will be a better place. Who knows when little "ripples" may turn into tidal waves, or …a national holiday!

Thank you, Captain Denny Flanagan, for being the inspiration for this book, and a wonderful example for the rest of us to follow!

To a Better World,

Mac Anderson
Founder, Simple Truths

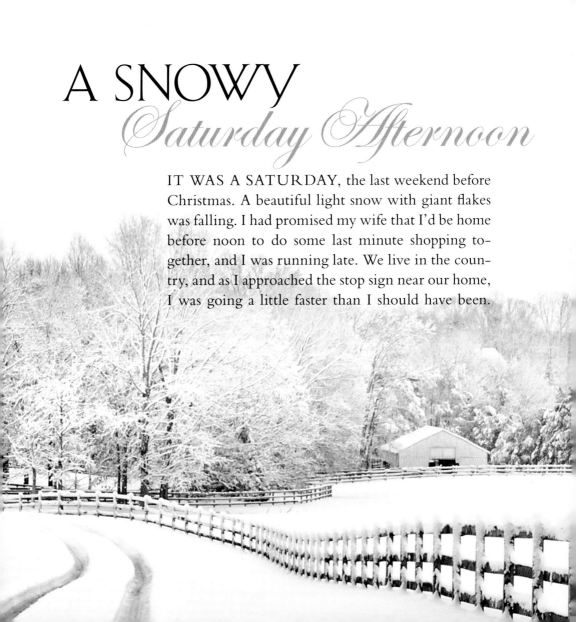

A SNOWY
Saturday Afternoon

IT WAS A SATURDAY, the last weekend before Christmas. A beautiful light snow with giant flakes was falling. I had promised my wife that I'd be home before noon to do some last minute shopping together, and I was running late. We live in the country, and as I approached the stop sign near our home, I was going a little faster than I should have been.

When I touched the brakes to stop, I didn't realize that under the snow was a layer of ice. And you can probably guess the rest of the story. The car slid through the intersection into a small ditch on the other side of the road.

We've all been there. I could see it happening in slow motion while thinking…the result will not be good! And, of course, I was right. Once the car entered the ditch, there was no getting out. I wasn't hurt, but I was angry with myself. I should have known better. A day that was supposed to be "Christmas fun" would be spent waiting for a tow truck to pull me out of the ditch.

The good news was that I was not far from my home, so I started walking to share the "no shopping today" news with my wife.

As I walked the short distance down our country road, I noticed two men who were building my neighbor's barn and I thought that maybe…just maybe, I could pay them to take a break and try to push me out.

What the heck, it was worth a shot, although I had serious doubts that "pushing it out" was an option. As I approached, I introduced myself and pointed to the car in the distance. Without hesitating, they looked at each other and said, "We can solve that problem!" One of them said, "I'll get the chain and George, you can drive the backhoe down the road and we'll have it out in no time!" The backhoe…I hadn't considered that, and the "hope factor" went up a notch.

In the next 30 minutes while I watched helplessly from the sidelines, they had my car out of the ditch and on the road again. To say that I was grateful was an understatement. My Saturday had been saved thanks to two men I'd never met before.

I thanked them, reached into my wallet and handed them a $100 bill. I said, "Please take this. It would have cost me more to call a tow truck and I would have spent my afternoon waiting for it to show." They both looked at me, and at the same time said, "No way! We wouldn't consider taking a cent." Then the one man said, "This was our good deed for the day and we know that you'll help someone else because we helped you. That's all we ask."

I drove away with a wonderful feeling inside, knowing there are people like this in the world. It made my day! But here's the amazing thing about kindness...from the look on their faces, it made theirs too! Emerson was so right when he said, "One of the most beautiful compensations in life is that no man can help another without helping himself." That afternoon in the mall I found myself looking for a few more doors to open, and moved a little faster to pick up a package dropped by an elderly lady. I had been reminded, once again, of the beauty and the power of kindness.

"THOSE WHO BRING
SUNSHINE INTO THE LIVES
OF OTHERS CANNOT KEEP
IT FROM THEMSELVES."

~JAMES BERRIE

Kurtis THE STOCK BOY *and Brenda* THE CHECKOUT GIRL

~JEFF GORDON, "Faith Guides Warner's Fate."
St. Louis Post-Dispatch.

IN A SUPERMARKET, Kurtis, the stock boy was busily working when a new voice came over the loud speaker asking for a carryout at register four. Kurtis was almost finished and wanted to get some fresh air, so he decided to answer the call. As he approached the check-out stand, a distant smile caught his eye; the new check-out girl was beautiful.

Later that day after his shift was over, he waited by the punch clock to find out her name. She came into the break room, smiled softly at him, took her card, punched out and left. He looked at her card, BRENDA.

He walked out only to see her start walking up the road. Next day, he waited outside as she left the supermarket and offered her a ride home. He looked harmless enough and she accepted. When he dropped her off, he asked if maybe he could see her again, outside of work. She simply said it wasn't possible.

He pressed and she explained that she had two children and couldn't afford a babysitter, so he offered to pay for the sitter. Reluctantly, she accepted his offer for a date the following Saturday. That Saturday night he arrived at her door only to have her tell him that she was unable to go. The babysitter had called and canceled. To which Kurtis simply said, "Well, let's take the kids with us."

She tried to explain that taking the children was not an option, but again, not taking no for an answer, he pressed. Finally, Brenda brought him inside to meet her children. She had an older daughter who was just as cute as a bug, Kurtis thought. Then Brenda brought out her son in a wheelchair. He was born a paraplegic with Down syndrome.

Kurtis asked Brenda, "I still don't understand why the kids can't come with us?" Brenda was amazed. Most men would run away from a woman with two kids, especially if one had disabilities—just like her first husband and father of her children had done. Kurtis was not ordinary—he had a different mindset.

That evening Kurtis and Brenda loaded up the kids, went to dinner and the movies. When her son needed anything, Kurtis took care of him. When he needed to use the restroom, he picked him up out of his wheelchair, took him and brought him back. The kids loved Kurtis. At the end of the evening,

Brenda knew this was the man she was going to marry and spend the rest of her life with.

A year later, they were married and Kurtis adopted both of her children. Since then they have added two more.

So what happened to Kurtis, the stock boy, and Brenda the check-out girl? Well, Mr. & Mrs. Kurt Warner now live in Arizona, where he was employed as the quarterback of the National Football League Arizona Cardinals. Is this a surprise ending or could you have guessed that he was not an ordinary person? It should be noted that Kurt Warner also quarterbacked the Rams in Super Bowl XXXVI. He has also been the NFL's Most Valuable Player twice and the Super Bowl's Most Valuable Player.

I love great stories with happy endings!

THE HIGHWAY
of Life

SAM FOSS (1858-1911) was a popular journalist, humorist and poet. He was widely published in newspapers and quite successful with his lectures and readings. His most noted written work was created from an experience he had on a humid summer day while taking a walk in the country and becoming lost in thought.

With the sun blazing down on him, he suddenly realized how hot and tired he was. He noticed a big tree at the side of the road, so he stopped for a moment to rest in the shade. Then he saw a little sign on the tree that read, "There is a good spring inside the fence. Come and drink if you are thirsty."

Foss climbed over the fence, found and enjoyed the cool water, and then read another sign attached to a bench, "Sit down and rest awhile if you are tired." Now thoroughly delighted and intrigued, he saw a barrel of apples nearby, which was accompanied by yet another sign. "If you like apples, just help yourself." He picked out a plump red apple, bit into it, and then looked up to see an elderly man watching him.

"I'm glad you dropped by," the host told Foss. The grateful traveler then asked about the signs and the gifts. The elderly man explained that the flowing water was going to waste, the bench had been gathering dust in his attic, and he had more apples in his orchard than he could possibly use. He went on to say that he and his wife had decided it would be neighborly to offer tired, thirsty passersby a place to rest and refresh themselves. He said that in doing so they had made a host of new friends.

"You must really like people," Foss responded to the explanation. "Of course," the elderly man replied. "Don't you?" Later, as Foss thought about the pleasant encounter, he remembered a line from Homer's *Iliad* that read, "He was a friend of man, and lived in a house by the side of the road." From his personal experience and the line from Homer, a poem began to take shape. He titled his now-famous poem, "The House by the Side of the Road," and here are some of the lines:

"I see from my house by the side of the road—by the side of the highway of life—the men who press on with ardor of hope—the men who are faint with strife—but I turn not away from their smiles nor their tears—both part of an infinite plan—let me live in a house by the side of the road—and be a friend to man."

A TREE IS KNOWN BY ITS
FRUIT; A MAN BY HIS DEEDS.
A GOOD DEED IS NEVER LOST;
HE WHO SOWS COURTESY
REAPS FRIENDSHIP, AND HE
WHO PLANTS KINDNESS
GATHERS LOVE.

~SAINT BASIL

Someone
WHO CARES

THIS IS A WONDERFUL STORY. I don't know who wrote it, but it captures the essence of caring, kindness and love.

It was a busy morning, approximately 8:30 am, when an elderly gentleman in his 80s arrived to have stitches removed from his thumb. He stated that he was in a hurry, as he had an appointment at 9:00 a.m.

I took his vital signs and had him take a seat, knowing it would be over an hour before someone would be able to see him. I saw him looking at his watch and decided, since I was not busy with another patient, I would evaluate his wound.

KINDNESS

Upon examination it was well healed, so I talked to one of the doctors, got the needed supplies to remove his sutures and redress his wound. While taking care of his wound, we began to engage in conversation. I asked him if he had a doctor's appointment this morning, as he was in such a hurry. The gentleman told me no, that he needed to go to the nursing home to eat breakfast with his wife.

I then inquired as to her health. He told me that she had been there for a while and that she was a victim of Alzheimer's disease. As we talked and I finished dressing his wound, I asked if she would be worried if he was a bit late. He replied that she no longer knew who he was, that she had not recognized him for five years now.

I was surprised and asked him, "And you still go every morning, even though she doesn't know who you are?" He smiled as he patted my hand and said, "She doesn't know me, but I still know who she is."

I had to hold back tears as he left. I had goose bumps on my arm, and thought, "That is the kind of love I want in my life." True love is neither physical nor romantic. True love is an acceptance of all that is, has been, will be, and will not be.

Pass It On!

KINDNESS IS LIKE a snowball that's rolling down a hill. Each unselfish act or word is another snowflake that greets the others…creating something much larger than itself in the process.

KINDNESS—PASS IT ON * By Maureen Weiner

I was standing at the station,
 Waiting for the train,
 Grumpy and bedraggled
 From running in the rain.

Fumbling with my backpack,
 Looking for my purse,
 Juggling all my parcels
 And trying not to curse.

A woman approached me
 With an out-stretched hand.
 I looked at her, quite puzzled:
 "I don't understand?"

As she handed me five dollars,
 Her pretty brown eyes shone.
 "Finally now I've got the chance
 To pass some kindness on!"

"You see, a little while ago,
 Things were really tough.
 A single mum with three young kids-
 There never was enough."

"I was shopping at the store one day,
 Trying not to cry.
 There wasn't enough money
 For what I had to buy."

Standing at the check-out,
 Not knowing what to do,
 When a young man waiting next to me
 Said: *"I'll get those for you."*

I felt so very humbled
 By the story that he told
 Of a deed that really changed his life
 When he was twelve years old.

He was lying in the hospital,
Very close to death.
Attached to drips and monitors,
Struggling for each breath.

His mother sat outside his room,
Her eyes were red from crying.
Trying hard to come to terms
Her precious son was dying.

A stranger sat beside her,
His face was tired and grey.
But what he had to say to her
Changed her life that day.

*"The doctors have done everything,
I know they really tried.
But now I am heart-broken-
My lovely Grace just died!*

*She was such a kindly soul,
And so, my darling wife,
Has given up her organs
So your boy won't lose his life.*

*The only thing I ask of you
Is to tell your precious son,
That, one day, when he has the chance,
To pass her kindness on."*

I took the money from her hand.
We shared a warm embrace.
The woman left me with,
A smile upon her face.

We all make excuses,
"I will...someday...somehow".
The question isn't where or when,
The time to act is now.

Labeling
CAN BE
DISABLING

IT WAS A COLD, WINDY DAY in Chicago. The time...6:00 a.m. The place...O'Hare Airport. The mood...tired!

I was going through airport security with 300 of my "closest friends." As I successfully walked through the scanner, I glanced to my right and one of the security guards was going through the bag of a young Arab man. For an instant, I remember thinking...I am glad they're checking that bag. Then I put on my shoes, gathered my belongings and headed down concourse B in the United terminal.

I had walked about a 100 yards when I heard someone running behind me and yelling, "Sir, Sir." I turned around to see the young Arab man with a smile on his face, as he handed me my laptop computer that I had left in the bin at security. He then said, "I thought you might need this!"

I thanked him over and over, but he said, "No problem, you would have probably done the same for me."

For as long as I live, I'll never forget that moment. We live in a complicated world where it can be easy to be afraid, and easy to be prejudiced. However, I truly feel that 99 percent of the people in the world, regardless of their skin color or religion, want to do the right thing. They want to be kind when given the opportunity. Therefore, we must always guard against allowing the one percent to sway our thinking. You may not know this, but almost every religion and every culture in the world, has one thing in common—they teach kindness as a virtue—not exactly the same words as the Golden Rule, but the same meaning.

The wonderful lesson that I "re-learned" that morning at the airport was this...labeling can be disabling. It was a lesson taught to me by an unexpected act of kindness...one I'll never forget!

No problem, you would have
probably done the same for me.

The Boomerang
EFFECT OF
Kindness

CALL IT KARMA or the laws of the universe, whatever kindness you share with others comes back to you. There's nothing like the feeling you get when you are kind to someone else…without the slightest expectation of anything in return.

"It is one of the most beautiful compensations in life that no man can sincerely try to help another without helping himself."

RALPH WALDO
EMERSON

In fact, taking the time to be kind can actually be good for your health. In his book, *The Healing Power of Doing Good: The Health and Spiritual Benefits of Helping Others*, Allan Luks documented the physical and mental benefits of kindness after surveying more than 3,000 volunteers of all ages at more than 20 organizations throughout the country.

Luks, the former executive director of the Institute for the Advancement of Health and executive director of Big Brothers/Big Sisters of New York City, shared some of the key findings from his study:

- A rush of euphoria, followed by a longer period of calm after performing a kind act, is often referred to as a "helper's high," involving physical sensations and the release of the body's natural painkillers, endorphins. This initial rush is then followed by a longer-lasting period of improved emotional well-being.

- Stress-related health problems improve after performing kind acts. Helping reverses feelings of depression, supplies social contact, and decreases feelings of hostility and isolation that can cause stress, overeating, ulcers, etc. A drop in stress may, for some people, decrease the constriction within the lungs that leads to asthma attacks.

- Helping can enhance our feelings of joyfulness, emotional resilience and vigor, and can reduce the unhealthy sense of isolation.

- A decrease in both the intensity and the awareness of physical pain can occur.

- The health benefits and sense of well-being return for hours or even days whenever the helping act is remembered.

- An increased sense of self-worth, greater happiness and optimism, as well as a decrease in feelings of helplessness and depression, is achieved.

BECAUSE
NICE MATTERS

"CARRY OUT A RANDOM ACT OF KINDNESS, WITH NO EXPECTATION OF REWARD, SAFE IN THE KNOWLEDGE THAT ONE DAY SOMEONE MIGHT DO THE SAME FOR YOU."

~PRINCESS DIANA

THE UNEXPECTED IS...
The Best

I RECENTLY READ an article where singer, Tony Bennett, shares how one act of kindness made a big difference in his life.

Here's what he said:

"I was going through a terrible divorce and my personal life was a mess. I goofed so bad. That Christmas I was in a hotel room by myself. It was the first time I'd ever spent the holidays away from family. All of a sudden, I heard some music. I opened the door to find one of the greatest surprises of my life: There was a choir singing 'On a Clear Day You Can See Forever.' My friend Duke Ellington, who happened to be in town for a concert, had heard I was alone.

So he sent a choir for me. For years, this kindness from Duke lifted up my whole life. It showed me that no matter how bad things seem, there are always people in this world who care about others.

That revelation changed my life."

"EVERY PERSON IN THIS LIFE
        HAS SOMETHING TO TEACH ME—
            AND AS SOON AS I ACCEPT THAT,
    I OPEN MYSELF TO TRULY LISTENING."

                        ~CATHERINE DOUCETTE

EVERY PERSON HAS
Something to Teach

FROM THE MOMENT we wake up each morning to the time we hit the pillow at night, we hear what people have to say, but are we really listening?

"To the world you may be just one person...but to one person you might just be the world."

MARK TWAIN

Really taking the time to hear what our spouses, children, co-workers, friends and neighbors are telling us can be one of the greatest acts of kindness. Having someone take the interest and time to really listen to what we're saying, validates us and makes us feel appreciated...no matter how old we are.

Robert Flack shared the following in an article in the San Antonio *Business Journal*:

"A 4-year-old girl felt her newspaper-reading father was ignoring her. After he said 'uh-huh' for the third time, she reached over, and pulled down the paper.

"Listen to me with your whole face!" she said.

An African proverb says it best, "One must talk little and listen much." Only when we take that sage wisdom to heart will kindness be spread through the silence of listening.

"TO GIVE WITHOUT ANY REWARD,
OR ANY NOTICE,
HAS A SPECIAL QUALITY OF ITS OWN."

~ANNE MORROW LINDBERGH

ICE CREAM
for the Soul

~AUTHOR UNKNOWN

LAST WEEK I took my children to a restaurant. My six-year-old son asked if he could say grace. As we bowed our heads he said, "God is good, God is great. Thank you for the food, and I would even thank you more if Mom gets us ice cream for dessert. And Liberty and justice for all! Amen!"

Along with the laughter from the other customers nearby, I heard a woman remark, "That's what's wrong with this country. Kids today don't even know how to pray. Asking God for ice cream! Why, I never!"

Hearing this, my son burst into tears and asked me, "Did I do it wrong? Is God mad at me?"

As I held him and assured him that he had done a terrific job and God was certainly not mad at him, an elderly gentleman approached the table.

He winked at my son and said, "I happen to know that God thought that was a great prayer." "Really?" my son asked. "Cross my heart," the man replied.

Then in a theatrical whisper he added (indicating the woman whose remark had started this whole thing), "Too bad she never asks God for ice cream. A little ice cream is good for the soul sometimes."

Naturally, I bought my kids ice cream at the end of the meal. My son stared at his for a moment and then did something I will remember for the rest of my life.

He picked up his sundae and without a word, walked over and placed it in front of the woman. With a big smile he told her, "Here, this is for you. Ice cream is good for the soul sometimes; and my soul is good already."

Sometimes we all need some ice cream.

www.gagirl.com (inspiring short stories)

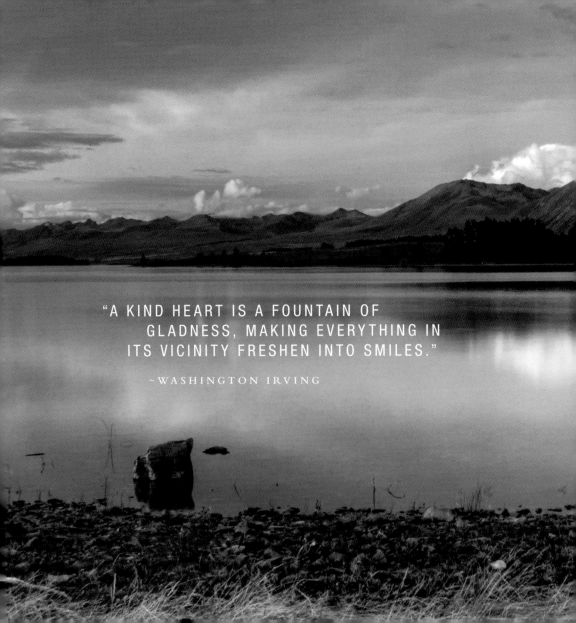

"A KIND HEART IS A FOUNTAIN OF
GLADNESS, MAKING EVERYTHING IN
ITS VICINITY FRESHEN INTO SMILES."

~WASHINGTON IRVING

Today
IS A GIFT

~PIERO FERRUCCI

"LIVING IN THE MOMENT"—It's a concept that challenges each of us to fully participate in life. Today's lifestyles are complex, cluttered and often confusing—leaving us struggling to balance our never-ending to-do list with planning for the future. But, taking a moment to be kind to those around us allows us to fully experience the only thing we really have—the present.

Speaker and Author Carl Mays shared a story he wrote with me that really illustrates why the time we spend with others is more important than anything else…

"Miss Esther's husband passed away years ago. I never met him even though I had known her for over twenty years before her recent death. Miss Esther's son was in his sixties and lived two thousand miles from her home in the Southern Highlands. She didn't see him much and talked with him infrequently on the phone. She had no other living relatives that anyone was aware of. Her few surviving friends were in their eighties or nineties and, like Miss Esther, didn't get out often. Some were in nursing homes. That's why my wife, Jean, and I decided to give her presents during the Christmas season—to let her know we were thinking of her.

I drove Jean to a local nursing home to visit her ailing mother. The plan then was for me to go by Miss Esther's house for a few minutes, give her the presents, and then come back to join Jean and her mother. My few minutes with Miss Esther turned into two hours.

We talked about a lot of things that afternoon, with Miss Esther doing most of the talking. I suppose I egged her on with questions, but she relished them and enjoyed answering in-depth. She told me about the first Christmas she remembered as a little girl and how she, her brothers and sisters each got an orange, apple, and some stick candy. Fruit was a special treat and candy was almost unheard of except during the holidays. She said Christmas always held a magical quality for her as she was growing up, regardless of how hard the times were or how little she received.

She described the first Christmas she and her husband, Abner, spent together. It was in a one-room cabin on a mountain farm. She took care of most of the farming and Abner worked long and hard at a lumber company. She said she could still recall the fresh smell of the Christmas tree they cut, dragged into their home and decorated.

'Mercy,' she exclaimed, 'living in that little cabin during the holidays was like camping in the woods except the pine fragrance was stronger inside because it was so contained in that small space!'

Miss Esther talked about how her son, Matthew, had served in the military and then worked in electronics, but she didn't know exactly what he did in either occupation. And even though he didn't get home or phone her much, he sent cards and gifts on special occasions. His marriage ended in an early divorce and he never remarried, but he was dating a divorcee with a couple of grown children. Matthew never had children of his own, and she hated that because she would have had loved to have a grandchild or two.

But the thing I remember most about my visit with Miss Esther was her poignant remark as I was departing. There was a glow on her face, excitement in her expression, and sparkling moisture in her eyes as she touched me with her words:

'I want to thank you again
for your presents—but I want to thank you
even more for your presence.'

As I drove away, I remained fixated on her unforgettable look and soul-stirring words—the last words I ever heard her speak."

In his book, **The Power of Kindness, the Unexpected Benefits of Leading a Compassionate Life**, psychologist Piero Ferrucci describes the importance of "being present" for those we come in contact with every day:

"To be in the present with someone else is a gift. The gift of attention is perhaps the most precious and envied of all, even though we do not always realize it. To be there. To be totally available. This is what we secretly hope other people will do for us, and we know it will give us healing relief, space, energy."

"Yesterday is history.
Tomorrow is a mystery. But today is God's gift.
That is why it is called the present."

JOAN RIVERS

"FOR BEAUTIFUL EYES, LOOK FOR THE GOOD IN OTHERS; FOR BEAUTIFUL LIPS, SPEAK ONLY WORDS OF KINDNESS; AND FOR POISE, WALK WITH THE KNOWLEDGE THAT YOU ARE NEVER ALONE."

~AUDREY HEPBURN

MAKE ME FEEL
Important

Mary Kay Ash was the inspirational founder of Mary Kay Cosmetics. Many years ago I heard her speak to a group of executives, and she told of her first sales job when she was in her early 20s. She had been excited because she was attending her first convention, and was going to get to meet the top sales person of the company. At a reception, she made her way through the crowd, introduced herself, and asked the man to please share some of his secrets to success. And, do you know what he said? Absolutely nothing! He just walked away.

> ## "WHEREVER THERE IS A HUMAN BEING, THERE IS A OPPORTUNITY FOR A KINDNESS."
>
> ~ SENECA

Mary Kay said it was a defining moment in her life, and she promised herself that if she ever enjoyed any success in her life, she would share it with others. Once she started her own company, she said when she walked into a room she would pretend that everyone had a sign around their neck that said...MAKE ME FEEL IMPORTANT.

We all want to feel important, and one of the simplest acts of kindness, one of the simplest ways to make anyone feel important is to sincerely listen to what they have to say.

My friend, Jim Cathcart, has a wonderful definition for listening. He said, "Listening is wanting to hear." All my life, I've noticed that people who are kind, truly want to hear.

"Never let loyalty and kindness get away from you! Wear them like a necklace; write them deep within your heart."

PROVERBS 3:3

The Elf On
CHRISTMAS DAY

JUST LIKE STANDING at the ocean's shore, when we're passing through life, we only see the surface. Oftentimes, there's a storm brewing beneath what people show to the world every day. That's why the Power of Kindness is so profound. While you may not know it, when you reach out in kindness, its soothing comfort can make the recipient feel a spark of hope and a connection to others just when they're needed most.

Lisa Tamburino told me a story about how you really never know what people are struggling with…and the impact your kindness can have. Lisa is a waitress at a restaurant in Naperville, Illinois, and got in the festive spirit of the holidays by donning an elf costume on Christmas Day.

"While I was serving my tables, a gentleman from another part of the restaurant wanted to randomly pick out a table and buy that table their meal. That table happened to be one of my tables and when the couple I was serving found out that someone had bought their meal, they called me over and were very appreciative. They wanted to pay it forward and told me to then give them the check from my other table where a man and his two little girls were having their Christmas breakfast.

"I thought it was a wonderful gesture and respected their wishes and waited until they were gone to surprise the gentleman and his two little girls. I let him know that he did not have a check for his meal. He looked at me like I just gave him a million dollars. I told him a couple that was sitting at the booth by the window bought their breakfast and he questioned why. I told him it was a couple that just wanted to pay it forward.

"His eyes starting tearing up and he told me that he had lost his business, his house and that he could barely afford to take his girls out to breakfast. I started to tear up, seeing what this gesture meant to him. After listening to the struggles he was having, I told him not to leave me a gratuity of any kind. I wanted him to walk out of the restaurant without pulling a dime out of his pocket and I gave his two little girls the Andes Candies box I had in my apron. They were so happy. Their dad told me it was their favorite candy. We had a long conversation and as they were leaving, the older of the two little girls got up and hugged me. It completely touched my heart."

"*May you remember that love flows best
when it flows freely, and it is in giving
that we receive the greatest gift.*"

KATE NOWAK

A Special Valentine

By Maureen Weiner

The playground was a-flutter
With giggles everywhere.
Young girls in huddles, whispering,
And love was in the air.

Cupid was on stand-by
With lovers in his sight,
Bow and arrow poised and ready
For a magic flight.

The little boy approached his mom,
A football in his hand,
Scruffy knees and dirty pants
From playing in the sand.

He stood beside her awkwardly,
A flush rose to his cheek,
Nervously he cleared his throat—
"Mom, we need to speak!"

It's Valentine's tomorrow
And I need to buy a card.
I need a woman's help with this—
For me it's just too hard.

The mother felt a little smile
Creep up on her face.
Her little boy was growing up
At such a rapid pace.

"So who's the lucky girl?" she asked,
A twinkle in her eyes,
The answer that he gave her
Really took her by surprise.

"Everyone has chosen
Who'll be their Valentine,
And sent them cards and flowers
That say, *Please will you be mine.*

But there's a new girl in our class,
She's just come to our school,
And no-one really likes her
Because she isn't cool.

You see, she isn't pretty,
And she isn't very smart.
When she finds she's been left out
It's going to hurt her heart."

The mother took her little son
To find the perfect gift.
To choose a special card they knew
Would give the girl a lift.

Looking through the cards that day
The mother took her time
To find the deepest meaning
Behind that Valentine.

She learnt about compassion,
About humanity.
She learnt about true kindness
From a boy with muddy knees.

THE
INCALCULABLE
Estate

I ONCE HEARD SOMEONE SAY, "If you teach your children the Golden Rule, you will have left them an incalculable estate." Truer words were never spoken.

More than anything, the Golden Rule is about kindness. John Blumberg, author, speaker and friend, recently told me a story that I'd like to share with you:

I had just experienced a pleasant flight from New York back to Chicago on United Airlines. It was one of those days where almost everything had gone right. That's until I exited the tram to the airport's economy parking lot and realized that I had lost my wallet on my homeward journey.

Throughout the drive home I mentally started retracing my steps. Once home, I placed calls to the "lost-and-found" at O'Hare, United, NY-LaGuardia and the TSA security in New York. At that late night hour I got recordings, so I left each a detailed message. I then retired to bed knowing I had done all I could do. I fell asleep thinking of the hassle of replacing everything in the wallet.

The next morning, I had been up for less than an hour when a man called. Bob identified himself with United Airlines, and his question was music to my ears—"Mr. Blumberg, are you missing a wallet?" Relieved and grateful, I responded, "YES!" I thanked him for returning my call to United's lost-and-found. But he didn't know about that call. He wasn't with the lost-and-found— nor was it his job to personally follow-up with passengers leaving their stuff on the airplane. He was the night mechanic who had simply found the wallet on my assigned seat. Realizing my phone number was not anywhere in my wallet, I immediately appreciated his extra effort of tracking down my home phone number. But that effort was only the beginning of what I was about to experience.

Bob had waited the night to call, assuming I would be sleeping. He told me that he was leaving work at 7:00 a.m. He wanted to know if I would be home so he could deliver my wallet to my house on his way home. After talking logistics for a minute, I realized that he was going over an hour out of his way. But he insisted. I finally got him to agree that I would immediately leave and meet him in a direction near his home. For the next 45 minutes, we both drove towards a common meeting place.

We finally met in the parking lot of a commercial building. As I got out of my car to meet this stranger-turned-hero, I introduced myself to Bob. He sported his heavy United Airlines uniform coat made necessary by the cold December morning. He greeted me with a big smile and handed me my wallet. I pulled some cash from my pocket to give him a sizeable tip for all his efforts. As I reached to hand him the cash, he didn't miss a beat. He simply responded, "Absolutely not!"

Bob continued, "I have lost my wallet before and I know it is a hassle. I am just glad that I could get it back to you." Feeling the need to somehow respond to his kindness, I offered the tip a couple more times. But he was not budging. Realizing the tip minimized his graciousness, I just smiled and said, "I guess I will just have to pay-it-forward to someone else." He smiled, "That would be great." You see, Bob went the extra mile...and then some. He didn't do it for gain, he did it simply because it's who he is.

"AFTER THE VERB 'TO LOVE'...
'TO HELP' IS THE MOST
BEAUTIFUL VERB IN THE WORLD."

~BERTHA VON SUTTNER

Anyway

People are unreasonable, illogical, self-centered...
Love them anyway.

If you do good, people will accuse you of selfish ulterior
Motives...do good anyway.

If you are successful, you win false friends and true
Enemies...be successful anyway.

The good you do today may be forgotten tomorrow...
Do good anyway.

Honesty and frankness will make you vulnerable...
Be honest and frank anyway.

[CONTINUED]

People love underdogs but follow only top dogs...
Follow some underdogs anyway.

What you spend years building may be destroyed overnight...
Build anyway.

People really need help, but attack you if you try to help...
Help them anyway.

Give the world the best you have...you may get kicked in the teeth,
But give the world the best you have anyway!

You see, in the final analysis, it's between you and God.
It was never between you and them anyway.

＊ *(Anonymous: found in Mother Teresa's Calcutta office)*

"THE FRAGRANCE ALWAYS
STAYS IN THE HAND THAT
GIVES THE ROSE."

~GEORGE WILLIAM CURTIS

THE POWER OF
Encouragement

~WRITTEN BY SCOTT ADAMS—*creator of Dilbert*

IN JANUARY OF 1986, I was flipping through the channels on TV and saw the closing credits for a PBS show called, "Funny Business," a show about cartooning. I had always wanted to be a cartoonist but never knew how to go about it. I wrote to the host of the show, cartoonist Jack Cassady, and asked his advice on entering the profession.

A few weeks later I got an encouraging handwritten letter from Jack, answering all of my specific questions about materials and process. He went on to warn me about the likelihood of being rejected at first, advising me not to get discouraged if that happened. He said the cartoon samples I sent him were good and worthy of publication.

I got very excited, finally understanding how the whole process worked. I submitted my best cartoons to *Playboy* and *The New Yorker.* The magazines quickly rejected me with cold little photocopied form letters. Discouraged, I put my art supplies in the closet and decided to forget about cartooning.

In June of 1987—out of the blue—I got a second letter from Jack Cassady. This was surprising, since I hadn't even thanked him for the original advice. Here's what his letter said:

> *Dear Scott:*
>
> *I was reviewing my "Funny Business" mail file when I again ran across your letter and copies of your cartoons. I remember answering your letter.*
>
> *The reason I'm dropping you this note is to again encourage you to submit your ideas to various publications. I hope you have already done so and are on the road to making a few bucks and having some fun too.*
>
> *Sometimes encouragement in the funny business of graphic humor is hard to come by. That's why I am encouraging you to hang in there and keep drawing.*
>
> *I wish you lots of luck, sales and good drawing.*
>
> *Sincerely,*
> *Jack*

I was profoundly touched by his letter, largely I think, because Jack had nothing to gain—including my thanks, if history was any indication. I acted on his encouragement, dragged my art supplies out of storage and inked the sample strips that eventually became Dilbert. Now, 700 newspapers and six books later, things are going pretty well in Dilbertville.

I feel certain that I wouldn't have tried cartooning again if Jack hadn't sent the second letter. With a kind word and a postage stamp, he started a chain of events that reaches all the way to you right now. As Dilbert became more successful, I came to appreciate the enormity of Jack's simple act of kindness. I did eventually thank him, but I could never shake the feeling that I had been given a gift which defied reciprocation. Somehow, "thanks" didn't seem to be enough.

Over time I have come to understand that some gifts are meant to be passed on, not repaid.

I expect at least a million people to read this newsletter. Each of you knows somebody who would benefit from a kind word. I'm encouraging you to act on it before the end of the year. For the biggest impact, do it in writing. And do it for somebody who knows you have nothing to gain. It's important to give encouragement to family and friends, but their happiness and yours are inseparable. For the maximum impact, I'm suggesting that you give your encouragement to someone who can't return the favor—it's a distinction that won't be lost on the recipient. And remember there's no such thing as a small act of kindness. Every act creates a ripple with no logical end.

~SCOTT ADAMS—*creator of Dilbert*

a kind word

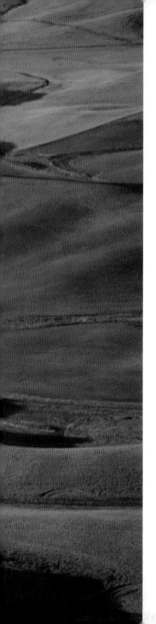

WHO PACKED
Your Parachute?

~BY TOM MATHEWS

CHARLES PLUMB was a U.S. Navy jet pilot in Vietnam. After 75 combat missions, his plane was destroyed by a surface-to-air missile. Plumb ejected and parachuted into enemy hands. He was captured and spent six years in a communist Vietnamese prison. He survived the ordeal and now lectures on lessons learned from that experience!

One day, when Plumb and his wife were sitting in a restaurant, a man at another table came up and said, "You're Plumb! You flew jet fighters in Vietnam from the aircraft carrier Kitty Hawk. You were shot down!"

"How in the world did you know that?" asked Plumb.

"I packed your parachute," the man replied. Plumb gasped in surprise and gratitude. The man pumped his hand and said, "I guess it worked!" Plumb assured him, "It sure did. If your chute hadn't worked, I wouldn't be here today."

Plumb couldn't sleep that night, thinking about that man. Plumb says, "I kept wondering what he had looked like in a Navy uniform: a white hat; a bib in the back; and bell-bottom trousers. I wonder how many times I might have seen him and not even said, 'Good morning, how are you?' or anything because, you see, I was a fighter pilot and he was just a sailor." Plumb thought of the many hours the sailor had spent at a long wooden table in the bowels of the ship, carefully weaving the shrouds and folding the silks of each chute, holding in his hands each time the fate of someone he didn't know.

Now, Plumb asks his audience, "Who's packing your parachute?" Everyone has someone who provides what they need to make it through the day. He also points out that he needed many kinds of parachutes when his plane was shot down over enemy territory—he needed his physical parachute, his mental parachute, his emotional parachute, and his spiritual parachute. He called on all these supports before reaching safety.

Sometimes in the daily challenges that life gives us, we miss what is really important. We may fail to say hello, please, or thank you, congratulate someone on something wonderful that has happened to them, give a compliment, or just do something nice for no reason. As you go through this week, this month, this year, don't forget to recognize the people who pack your parachutes.

"I CAN LIVE FOR
TWO MONTHS ON
A GOOD COMPLIMENT."

~MARK TWAIN

CHICAGO'S GENEROSITY
Not Forgotten

(A LETTER TO THE EDITOR—*Chicago Sun Times*)

My church (Shreveport Bible Church) had a youth mission trip to Chicago. I was one of the youth sponsors. We brought a group of high schoolers to do some inner-city work. In this case, we primarily worked with McCosh Elementary School, as well as one of the homeless shelters.

After working with one of the shelters, we were told that each leader would take two kids from our group and immerse ourselves in the city. Our goal was to take only $3 between us and to try and provide ourselves with a warm meal. You can imagine how I felt with two boys (my son, Quinn, and his friend, Brad Goodwin), as we were dropped downtown and told to fend for ourselves if we wanted to eat dinner.

Hence, we took to the streets and came upon a place where I saw the biggest, juiciest steaks and the most mouth-watering, deep-dish, Chicago-style pizza we had ever seen. More so because we were incredibly hungry and we knew there was no way we'd be able to enjoy these delectable morsels.

Well, I told the guys we were going into Ronny's Steakhouse to explain our dilemma. Basically, I walked in and told a gentleman I assumed was either the owner or the manager (I apologize for not remembering his name) that the three of us were very hungry and we would enjoy eating there very much; however, we only had $3 between all of us, and not a penny more. I asked him how much three slices of pizza cost. Now, the prices were clearly posted and the total we had wouldn't even come close to paying the taxes. He looked at me…then at the boys…and answered, "Three bucks." "How much if we included a salad?" I asked. Once again, he said, "Three bucks." "And some drinks?" I added. Again, "Three bucks. That's it. Anything you want to eat or drink here is three bucks total."

I gave him an understanding nod as I looked at the boys and said, "Grab some plates, we're eating at Ronny's!" Both boys, who have turned into fine young men, were given an impression that will last a lifetime. They were amazed at the generosity displayed to us in a city that has a reputation of being cold and uncaring. This quickly became the best pizza, salad and drinks the three of us had ever eaten before, or since—more so because we knew this was given out of graciousness to three total strangers.

At the end of our meal, I asked if we could please wash dishes and clear tables to show our appreciation. I was quickly told that we weren't allowed to work for our food and that this was given with no intention of getting anything in return. With that, we were given a bagful of plate-sized cookies and sent on our way. Our bellies were full of food and tears welled up in my eyes as we exited.

Even as I write this letter, I think about how much this show of kindness is so rare. Yet, three guys found the true spirit of Christmas, tucked away in the hustle and bustle of one of the largest and busiest cities in the world during a summer in your town. "Peace on Earth, good will toward men" manifested itself before our very eyes that day.

I'm sorry it took so long to get the word out about the generosity shown to us. This summer, I'll return to Chicago with my son and hopefully Brad, as our youth group will once again serve in your city. You can bet I'll be paying a visit to Ronny's Steakhouse downtown.

To all the people in Chicago, I pray for all of you during this season and through-out the rest of the year. May you show the true spirit of Christmas to each other and come see us in Shreveport, LA. You'll always have a friend here.

~KIP CUMMINGS—*Shreveport, LA*

FOREVER

Love NOT EXPRESSED *is Love* NOT RECEIVED

~JOANNE PATEK

MY HUSBAND AND I were married 30 years before he died suddenly from a heart attack. At that particular time in our lives, we were trying to pay cash for everything and get out of debt. His 280Z blew the engine and he was riding the bus to work while we saved for that engine repair.

Pat was an extraordinary man and dedicated husband, father, son, friend, and pastor to many. He would call me three times throughout the day and take the time to say, "I only have a fleeting moment and I wanted to give it to you, by saying how much I love you." On this one particular phone call, he was talking longer and even lamenting with a whine. "How fast can we get the budget to move so that I can drive again?" he asked me.

After his call, I asked myself what fun thing I could do to show support and love for him in order to encourage and lift his spirits. I then proceeded to take my lunch, go to Walgreens, get a box of chalk and drive eight blocks from our house to where the bus left him off each day.

With that chalk I drew big hearts on the street poles and sidewalk for all eight blocks and wrote the words, "Pat & Joanne Forever…True love to infinity and beyond…until the twelfth of never—forever I will be loving you."

On Pat's delightful walk home that evening, my LOVE was expressed all over for ALL to see, and it even stayed there for over a week for him to enjoy each evening as he emerged from the bus. I am so glad that I took the time to express myself so extravagantly, not knowing that he would die unexpectedly just a couple of months after that.

We never know when it is the last kiss or hug that we will get, so we try to never forget the power of each moment. Our family motto has always been, "Love not expressed is love not received." You can say you love me, but without expressing that love, I do not know it. I am so glad that I took the time to make that memory into a Kodak moment that day. What a lunch, and oh, what feeling it gave to both of us.

"YOU NEVER KNOW
    WHEN YOU'RE MAKING
A MEMORY."

~RICKIE LEE JONES

"I EXPECT TO PASS THROUGH LIFE BUT ONCE. IF, THEREFORE, THERE MAY BE ANY KINDNESS I CAN SHOW, OR ANY GOOD THING I MAY DO TO ANY FELLOW BEING, LET ME DO IT NOW AND NOT DEFER OR NEGLECT IT, AS I SHALL NOT PASS THIS WAY AGAIN."

~WILLIAM PENN

RANDOM ACTS
of Kindness

(EXCERPT FROM *Random Acts of Kindness*)

"WHEN I GRADUATED from college I took a job at an insurance company in this huge downtown office building. On my first day, I was escorted to this tiny cubicle surrounded by what seemed like thousands of other tiny cubicles, and put to work doing some meaningless thing. It was so terribly depressing I almost broke down crying. At lunch—after literally punching out on a time clock—all I could think about was how much I wanted to quit, but I couldn't because I desperately needed the money.

"When I got back to my cubicle after lunch there was a beautiful bouquet of flowers sitting on my desk. For the whole first month I worked there, flowers just kept arriving on my desk. I found out later that it had been a kind of spontaneous office project. A woman in the cubicle next to me brought in the first flowers to try to cheer me up, and then other people just began replenishing my vase. I ended up working there for two years, and many of my best, longest-lasting friendships grew out of that experience."

It's not how big our act of kindness is. It's the fact that we take the time to do it! We've all had good intentions—to make a dinner for someone struggling with an illness, to make a phone call to a friend we know could use it or remembering to be kind to an overworked salesclerk during a busy shopping day. But somehow, our intentions don't always become reality because we feel overwhelmed by all of the demands on our time.

Prioritizing your day will help you focus on the things you think are truly important. But, often your "to-do" list still seems overwhelming. If that's the case, it's time to change your attitude, not your tasks.

"The giving of love is an education in itself."

ELEANOR ROOSEVELT

Take an extra moment to focus on those around you...to do what you can. Practicing small acts of kindness doesn't even need to cost anything. Here are some other suggestions from *Random Acts of Kindness*:

- Put your shopping cart back in its appointed place in the parking lot.
- When someone is trying to merge into your lane in traffic, let him in—and why not smile and wave while doing it!
- Drop off a cutting from a houseplant to someone who might need a little beauty in his or her life.
- Write a note, along with your tip, thanking the person for something specifically. "Your smile as you served me dinner really made my day."
- Let the person in the grocery store line go ahead of you.
- Pay a toll for the car behind you.
- If you have an infirmed person living near you, offer to do the grocery shopping for him or her.
- If you know someone is going through a bad day or a difficult time in life, make it better by doing something—anything—to let him or her know someone cares...and don't let on who did it!

Those are a few ideas to get you started. Every day presents new opportunities to touch the lives of those around you!

Whether it's a Big Deed or
a Little One, just Do!

"KIND WORDS ARE A CREATIVE FORCE,
A POWER THAT CONCURS IN THE BUILDING
UP OF ALL THAT IS GOOD, AND ENERGY THAT
SHOWERS BLESSINGS UPON THE WORLD."

~LAWRENCE G. LOVASIK

TOUCHED BY A
Prayer

~MARTA W. ALDRICH, "Acts of Kindness"
American Profile

TRAVELING BY PLANE for the first time, the five-member Stieneke family of Cherokee, Iowa, was landing at Chicago's O'Hare airport when their 10-year-old son became upset and began to sob loudly.

"He was inconsolable," recalls Elaine Stieneke of her son, who has expressive language disorder and wailed for nearly 25 minutes once they reached the terminal.

Some passengers offered "advice," some sympathetic looks and others appeared disgusted and annoyed. However, one woman sat quietly watching, wiping away tears as she scribbled a note. She handed it to the flustered mom, who was too distraught to even acknowledge it.

Later on a connecting flight, Stieneke pulled out the note. It read:

> *"I've been there—not this exact situation but close enough. I asked God to give you everything good that I was going to receive today. The very best to you."*

"I cried like a baby when I read it," Stieneke says. "I was so overwhelmed by this message. It got me through that week and quite a few since then."

She keeps the crumpled paper tucked in her journal to remind her "there are a lot of good people out there."

"LIFE IS SHORT AND WE NEVER HAVE
ENOUGH TIME FOR GLADDENING
THE HEARTS OF THOSE WHO TRAVEL
THE WAY WITH US. OH, BE SWIFT
TO LOVE! MAKE HASTE TO BE KIND"

~HENRI FRÉDÉRIC AMIEL

"KINDNESS IS MORE IMPORTANT THEN WISDOM, AND THE RECOGNITION OF THIS IS THE BEGINNING OF WISDOM."

~THEODORE ISAAC RUBIN, MD

Lincoln...
WHAT WAS HE REALLY LIKE?

BEFORE HE BECAME PRESIDENT, Abraham Lincoln spent 20 years as an unsuccessful Illinois lawyer—at least he was unsuccessful in financial terms. But when you measure the good he did, he was very rich indeed. Legends are often untrue, but Lincoln was the real thing. During his years as a lawyer, there were hundreds of documented examples of his kindness, honesty and decency.

For example, Lincoln didn't like to charge people much who were as poor as he was. Once a man sent him $25, but Lincoln sent back ten of it, saying he was being too generous. He was known at times to convince his clients to settle their issue out of court, saving them a lot of money and earning himself nothing.

An old woman in dire poverty, the widow of a Revolutionary soldier was charged $200 for getting her $400 pension. Lincoln sued the pension agent and won the case for the old woman. He didn't charge her for his services and, in fact, paid her hotel bill and gave her money to buy a ticket home!

He and his associate once prevented a con man from gaining possession of a tract of land owned by a mentally ill girl. The case took 15 minutes. Lincoln's associate came to divide up their fee, but Lincoln reprimanded him. His associate argued that the girl's brother had agreed on the fee ahead of time, and he was completely satisfied. "That may be," said Lincoln, "but I am not satisfied. That money comes out of the pocket of a poor, demented girl; and I would rather starve than swindle her in this manner. You return half the money at least, or I'll not take a cent of it as my share."

Kindness and honesty make you feel good about yourself and create trust in others. They improve your relationship with yourself and with others. It's not much in fashion these days to talk about the benefits of kindness, honesty and decency, but the benefits are there and they are valuable and worth the trouble.

Lincoln didn't talk much about religion, even with his best friends, and he didn't belong to any church. But he once confided to a friend that his religious code was the same as an old man he knew in Indiana, who said, "When I do good, I feel good, and when I do bad, I feel bad, and that's my religion."

Paid IN FULL

ONE DAY, A POOR BOY who was selling goods from door-to-door to pay his way through school, found he had only one thin dime left, and he was hungry. He decided he would ask for a meal at the next house. However, he lost his nerve when a lovely young woman opened the door.

Instead of a meal, he asked for a drink of water. She thought he looked hungry and so she brought him a large glass of milk. He drank it slowly, and then asked, "How much do I owe you?"

"You don't owe me anything," she replied. "Mother has taught us never to accept pay for a kindness." He said, "Then I thank you from my heart." As Howard Kelly left that house, he not only felt stronger physically, but his faith in God and man was strengthened also. He had been ready to give up and quit.

strengthened

Years later, that young woman became critically ill. The local doctors were baffled. They finally sent her to the big city, where they called in specialists to study her rare disease.

Dr. Howard Kelly was called in for the consultation. When he heard the name of the town she came from, he went down the hall of the hospital to her room. Dressed in his doctor's gown, he went in to see her. He recognized her at once. He went back to the consultation room determined to do his best to save her life. From that day, he gave special attention to the case.

After a long struggle, the battle was won. Dr. Kelly requested from the business office to pass the final billing to him for approval. He looked at it, then wrote something on the edge, and the bill was sent to her room. She feared to open it, for she was sure it would take the rest of her life to pay for it all. Finally, she looked, and something caught her attention on the side of the bill. She read these words:

"Paid in full with one glass of milk..."

(Signed)
Dr. Howard Kelly

★ *Dr. Howard Kelly was a distinguished physician who, in 1895, founded the Johns Hopkins Division of Gynecologic Oncology at Johns Hopkins University. According to Dr. Kelly's biographer, Audrey Davis, the doctor was on a walking trip through Northern Pennsylvania one spring day when he stopped by a farm house for a drink of water.*

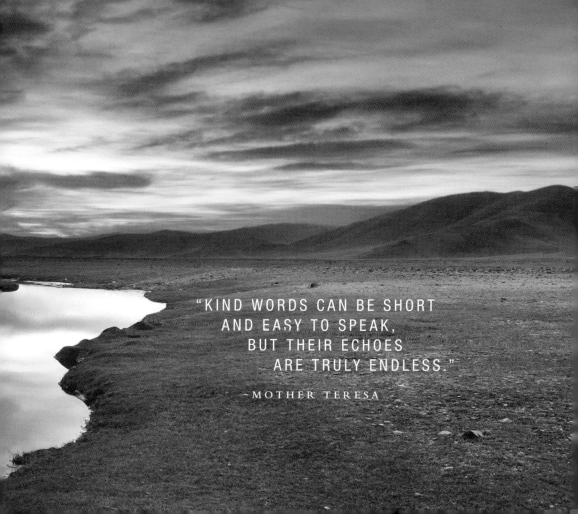

"KIND WORDS CAN BE SHORT
AND EASY TO SPEAK,
BUT THEIR ECHOES
ARE TRULY ENDLESS."

~MOTHER TERESA

Make a Difference
FOR A DAY...
Change the World
ALONG THE WAY

~BY MAC ANDERSON

Should I place a rose upon her desk
With a thank you note to say...
Your kindness is remembered,
You made a difference in my day.

Should I find the perfect card
And let my heart go wild?
Send it to the one I love
And for sure...ignite a smile.

Do I know a person who's in a bind?
Who could use a little love?
If I just listen, will I find...
A little help from above?

What if every soul would wake one morn
With courage standing tall?
Thinking I can make a difference...
Be it large or small.

For on that day, a spring of love would flow
Unlike we've ever seen.
Around the world, new hope would grow
Where indifference once had been.

And it would feel so good
In these times of pain and strife
That you just may decide...
To make a difference with your life.

So don't let another day go by
Without doing something kind.
The good you do will last forever,
And make a better world for yours and mine.

CONCLUSION

The great English writer, Aldous Huxley, was a pioneer in the study of philosophies and techniques to develop human potential. In a lecture toward the end of his life, he said this:

"People often ask me...what is the most effective technique for transforming their lives?"

He then said, "It's a little embarrassing that after years and years of research, my best answer is–**just be a little kinder.**"

This is the paradox of the power of kindness. It doesn't feel powerful at all. In fact, it almost feels too simple to be important. But as Huxley said, **it is the #1 thing that can transform your life.**

How can that be? Kindness and compassion are the principal things that make our lives meaningful. Although we don't often think about it, the truth is that these qualities are our primary source of joy and happiness. Why? Because these are the qualities from which so many other positive qualities flow such as **honesty**, **forgiveness**, **patience** and **generosity**. These qualities are the foundation of a good heart, and **with a good heart...a good life will follow.**

The Dalai Lama said this:

"My religion is kindness. I have found that the greatest degree of inner tranquility comes from the development of love and compassion. The more we care for the happiness of others, the greater our own sense of well-being. Cultivating a close, warm-hearted feeling for others automatically puts the mind at ease. It helps to remove whatever fears or insecurities we may have. It also gives us strength to cope with any obstacles we encounter. It is the principal source of success in life."

Kindness, more than anything, is an attitude that brings us back to the simplicity of being. It is also the one way you can be assured of making a difference with your life. If right now, at this moment, you make random acts of kindness a priority in your life, the world will be a better place and you'll be a happier person.

Here's to the difference you're going to make through the awesome power of kindness.

MAC ANDERSON
Founder, Simple Truths

"People often ask me...what is the most effective technique for transforming their lives?"

He then said, "It's a little embarrassing that after years and years of research, my best answer is— ***just be a little kinder.***"

ALDOUS HUXLEY

About the Author

MAC ANDERSON is the founder of Simple Truths and Successories, Inc., the leader in designing and marketing products for motivation and recognition. These companies, however, are not the first success stories for Mac. He was also the founder and CEO of McCord Travel, the largest travel company in the Midwest, and part owner/VP of sales and marketing for Orval Kent Food Company, the country's largest manufacturer of prepared salads.

His accomplishments in these unrelated industries provide some insight into his passion and leadership skills. He also brings the same passion to his speaking where he speaks to many corporate audiences on a variety of topics, including leadership, motivation, and team building.

Mac has authored or co-authored 14 books that have sold over three million copies. His titles include:

- *Change is Good . . . You Go First*
- *Charging the Human Battery*
- *Customer Love*
- *Finding Joy*
- *Learning to Dance in the Rain*
- *212°: The Extra Degree*
- *Motivational Quotes*
- *The Nature of Success*
- *The Power of Attitude*
- *The Essence of Leadership*
- *The Dash*
- *To a Child, Love is Spelled T-I-M-E*
- *You Can't Send a Duck to Eagle School*
- *What's the Big Idea?*

For more information about Mac, visit www.simpletruths.com